First World War
and Army of Occupation
War Diary
France, Belgium and Germany

25 DIVISION
74 Infantry Brigade
Durham Light Infantry
13th Battalion
1 September 1918 - 28 February 1919

WO95/2247/3

The Naval & Military Press Ltd
www.nmarchive.com
Published in association with The National Archives

Published by

The Naval & Military Press Ltd

Unit 10 Ridgewood Industrial Park,

Uckfield, East Sussex,

TN22 5QE England

Tel: +44 (0) 1825 749494

www.naval-military-press.com

www.nmarchive.com

This diary has been reprinted in facsimile from the original. Any imperfections are inevitably reproduced and the quality may fall short of modern type and cartographic standards.

© Crown Copyright
Images reproduced by permission of The National Archives, London, England, 2015.

Contents

Document type	Place/Title	Date From	Date To
Heading	WO95/2247-4		
Heading	13th Bn Durham Lt Infy Sep 1918-Feb 1919 From 23 Div. 68 Bde and Italy Same Div		
War Diary	In the field	01/09/1918	03/09/1918
War Diary	Mt Lemerle	04/09/1918	11/09/1918
War Diary	Centrale	12/09/1918	18/09/1918
War Diary	Striquier	19/09/1918	27/09/1918
War Diary	Ribemont	28/09/1918	28/09/1918
War Diary	Maricourt	29/09/1918	30/09/1918
War Diary	In the Line	01/10/1918	31/10/1918
War Diary	In the Field	01/11/1918	31/01/1919
War Diary	Villers-In Cauchies	01/02/1919	28/02/1919

WO95/2247/4

25TH DIVISION
74TH INFY BDE

13TH BN DURHAM LT INFY
SEP 1918 - FEB 1919

from 23 Div. 68 Bde
and ITALY same Div

Army Form C. 2118.

WAR DIARY
or
INTELLIGENCE SUMMARY.
(Erase heading not required.)

Place	Date	Hour	Summary of Events and Information	Remarks and references to Appendices

Army Form C. 2118.

WAR DIARY
INTELLIGENCE SUMMARY.
(Erase heading not required.)

PAGE 2 VOLUME 9
SEPTEMBER 1918

Place	Date	Hour	Summary of Events and Information	Remarks and references to Appendices
	5/9/18 contd		Three platoons on working parties	
	6/9/18		Three platoons on working parties. 2 Officers and 63 other ranks on fatigue. Remainder of men employed under Coy Commanders each in their section.	
	7/9/18		Very quiet day. 443 313 together brought 3 officers 741 other ranks Ration strength 25 " " 586	
	8/9/18		At 6 p.m. Battalion was ordered to move 15921 on night exercise. Of Light Divisional Front, at 9 p.m. roped ourselves.	
	9/9/18		Quiet day	
	10/9/18		Quiet day	
	14/9/18		Battalion relieved by 8th K.O.Y.L.I. Orders were received that this Battalion was to proceed to FRANCE forthwith. The Battalion proceeded to CENTRALE Railway for evening at N. PERONA Corner at CENTRALE at 10 p.m.	

WAR DIARY
INTELLIGENCE SUMMARY

Army Form C. 2118.

PAGE 3 VOLUME 9
SEPTEMBER 1918

Place	Date	Hour	Summary of Events and Information	Remarks and references to Appendices
CENTRALE	1/9/18		The G.O.C. Division and Brigade inspected Battalion. Orders were received that the Battalion proceed to THIENE in the 8th Div.	
	2/9/18		Coster equipment tak. Parade	
	3/9/18		A.F.B 213 Officers strength 3 officers 748 other ranks Ration Strength 33 " 780 "	
			The Battalion left CENTRALE in 2 sections	
			First half left at 9 a.m. and entrained at THIENE at 12 noon	
			Second half left at 2 p.m. and entrained at THIENE at 8 p.m.	
			First train arrived BOLOGNA 8.15 a.m. " " " 9.20 a.m.	
			The men had tea	
	4/9/18		Second train arrived BOLOGNA 2 a.m. left 5.40 a.m.	
			First train arrived VOGHERA 8.30 a.m. left " 10.10 a.m.	

Army Form C. 2118.

9th to 14th July
SEPTEMBER 1918

WAR DIARY
or
INTELLIGENCE SUMMARY.
(Erase heading not required.)

Instructions regarding War Diaries and Intelligence Summaries are contained in F. S. Regs., Part II. and the Staff Manual respectively. Title pages will be prepared in manuscript.

Place	Date	Hour	Summary of Events and Information	Remarks and references to Appendices
	13/9/18		Second train arrived VOGHERA 12.30 a.m.	
			left 1.30 a.m.	
			Troops had Tea	
			First train arrived SAN PIER D'ARENA 3.40 a.m.	
			left 4.52 a.m.	
			Second train arrived 7.0 a.m.	
			left 8.10 a.m.	
			Troops had Tea	
			First train arrived VENTIMIGLIA 2.30 a.m.	
			left 2.45 a.m.	
			Second train arrived 5.33 a.m.	
			left 6.03 a.m.	
	14/9/18		First train arrived CANNES 6.30 a.m.	
			left 7.15 a.m.	
			Second train arrived 11.0 a.m.	
			left 11.30 a.m.	
			Troops had Tea and dropped two patients	

Army Form C. 2118.

PAGE 1 Volume 9
SEPTEMBER 1918

WAR DIARY
or
INTELLIGENCE SUMMARY
(Erase heading not required.)

Instructions regarding War Diaries and Intelligence Summaries are contained in F. S. Regs., Part II. and the Staff Manual respectively. Title Pages will be prepared in manuscript.

Place	Date	Hour	Summary of Events and Information	Remarks and references to Appendices

Army Form C. 2118.

PH.H.C Mercery
SEPTEMBER 1918

WAR DIARY
or
INTELLIGENCE SUMMARY.
(Erase heading not required.)

Place	Date	Hour	Summary of Events and Information	Remarks and references to Appendices
	18/9/18		First Train arrived at RIVIER 4.30 A.M. and Marched to billets at MILLENCOURT arriving 7.30 A.M	
ST. RIVIER	19/9/18		Second Train arrived at RIVIER at 4 a.m by Battn marched to billets at MILLENCOURT arriving at 7.15 a.m	
	20/9/18		The G.O.C. 25th Division and 7th Infantry Brigade spoke to Battalion	
	21/9/18		The O.C. inspected the Battalion	
	22/9/18		Training and special march to keep Legs warmed (A.F.B.2.1) - Lectures Church to Officers J.O's N.C.O's Gas Lecture 2pm Musketry 7.30 ?	
	22/6/18		Church Parade	
	27/9/18		The C.O. Adjt and two Company Commanders marched to de Marie ridge Recce.	
	28/9/18 2pm		Received Warning Order to be ready to move when called on Convoy	
	29/9/18 4pm		Battn First Line Transport left and Companies by 9pm to HERMICOURT area	

Instructions regarding War Diaries and Intelligence Summaries are contained in F. S. Regs., Part II. and the Staff Manual respectively. Title pages will be prepared in manuscript.

WAR DIARY
or
INTELLIGENCE SUMMARY.
(Erase heading not required.)

Army Form C. 2118.

PAGE 7 VOLUME 6
SEPTEMBER 1918

Place	Date	Hour	Summary of Events and Information	Remarks and references to Appendices
	25/9/18 contd.		The Officers played the N.C.O's at Rugby football. Result N.C.O's 3 goals and 2 tries. Officers Nil.	
	26/9/18		All Lewis gunners fired on the range and the Battalion practised "Deploying" from column of route.	
	27/9/18	7am	Ref map ABBEVILLE 1a. The following transport left under 2/Lt [illegible]: 1 L.G. limber 4 [illegible] limbers 2 water carts 1 mess cart 3 Baggage wagons and 6 riders, and entrained at PONT REMY at 10.15 am arriving at CORBIE at 2 am 27th.	
		10.15 am	The Battalion marched to ST RIQUIER and entrained for ALBERT.	
RIBEMONT		6pm	The Battalion arrived at ALBERT and marched back to RIBEMONT arriving at 8.30 pm.	
	28/9/18	10am	The G.O.C. Division visited the Battalion.	
RIBEMONT	29/9/18	3am	Orders were received for the Battalion to move to MERICOURT.	
		10am	The Battalion left RIBEMONT and proceeded by bus to	

A5834 Wt. W4973/M687 750,000 8/16 D. D. & L. Ltd. Forms/C.2118/13.

Army Form C. 2118.

PAGE 8 VOLUME 9
SEPTEMBER 1918

WAR DIARY
or
INTELLIGENCE SUMMARY.
(Erase heading not required.)

Instructions regarding War Diaries and Intelligence Summaries are contained in F. S. Regs., Part II and the Staff Manual respectively. Title pages will be prepared in manuscript.

Place	Date	Hour	Summary of Events and Information	Remarks and references to Appendices
MARICOURT	29/9/18		Army at 3.30 a.m.	
	30/9/18	2/3	Officers Strength/Effectives 991 Other ranks Ration strength Inc. 720	
			The Original Prototypes the greater Rendezvous was Fullmont	

O.K. Crowder
COMDG 13TH (SERV.) Bn. DURHAM L.I. MTY

WAR DIARY
or
INTELLIGENCE SUMMARY

Army Form C. 2118.

Page 1 Volume 10 September 1918

Place	Date	Hour	Summary of Events and Information	Remarks and references to Appendices
Catelet	1/10/18	10 am	The Battalion left HARDECOURT AND BOIS and marched to MOISLAINS arriving at 2.30 am	
	2/10/18		The Battalion rested. R/M/f 6 o.c. - 6 o.r. 1/40 o.r.	
	3/10/18	1.15	The Battalion proceeded by march route to RONSOY. On the march orders were received to halt at RONSOY for 1/2 hr and proceed on to MT.S.MARTIN. Here the Battalion got into Battle Order and "B" Echelon moved back to F.21.a.2.d. Casualties 2 OR killed + 9 ORs wounded.	
	4/10/18		The Battalion rested at MT S.MARTINS.	
	5/10/18	At 1 am	the Battalion moved to assembly trenches east of PROSPECT HILL with object of attacking high ground N of BEAUREVOIR. Attack at first successful but Battalion had to retire owing to heavy casualties. Lt Colonel A BLAIR DSO. MC wounded. Capt. b W.B. Chapman, Lt. A.E Hale 7/Lt E.b.Forrest, R/Lt Robinson returned to duty. 2/Lt Gallows were wounded. Lt.s Lb.Smith + C.Dodd E S.R. Gallows were wounded. Lieut Hostert, + Lt Z. Andler "moving Battalion" again + Lieut J Golder were killed + Lt Z. Andler "moving Battalion" again moved forward but unable to advance far owing to very heavy M.G.fire. Line dug about 400 yds in advance of original starting point.	
	6/10/18		Advance continued. Sunken road BEAUREVOIR - VILLERS-OUTREAUX reached. 2/Lt W.R. Dewar wounded. Effective Strength 23 off 684 ORs Ration 18 604	

Army Form C. 2118.

Page 2 Volume 9
October 1918

WAR DIARY
or
INTELLIGENCE SUMMARY.
(Erase heading not required.)

Place	Date	Hour	Summary of Events and Information	Remarks and references to Appendices
Inthilui	9/10/18 & 8/10/18		Battalion dug in on sunken road BEAUREVOIR - VILLERS OUTREAUX. Relieved by 66th Division at 9 am on morning of 8th. Battn marched back to VORMISSET arriving there about 11 am. Here a good meal was obtained and remnants of Battn were cleaned up, washed & refitted with boots, flare etc.	
	9/10/18		At 2 am Battalion marched to SERRAIN FARM. Orders to attack were received on the march. Objective V.S. Central station P.9 a. About 2 pm Battalion was held up by O.N. railway embankment at 2 pm. Cavalry came up and Battalion advanced to final objective which was captured without much opposition. Capt J Rowley M.C. killed.	Sheet 57 B 5E
	10/10/18		At 8.30 am advance again resumed with objective high ground NE of LE CATEAU. Battalion held up on high ground S.W. of St BENIN at about 9 am. At 2.30 pm artillery barrage put down and Battalion again advanced captured village of St BENIN.	
	11/10/18		Here Battalion remained until relieved at 10 pm, on night of 11th by 2nd Munsters. After relief Battalion marched back to HONNECHY. Lt Col E A R Williams admitted Hospital	
			Total Casualties for operations 4th, 10 & 11th October	
			Officers. OR Killed 5 43 Wounded 15 311 Missing 1 74 21 428	

Army Form C. 2118.

WAR DIARY
or
INTELLIGENCE SUMMARY.

(Erase heading not required.)

Page 3 Volume 9.
October 1918

Instructions regarding War Diaries and Intelligence Summaries are contained in F. S. Regs., Part II. and the Staff Manual respectively. Title pages will be prepared in manuscript.

Place	Date	Hour	Summary of Events and Information	Remarks and references to Appendices
In the line	12/10/18		Battalion left Honnechy at 1.30 pm and marched to billets at PREMONT. Battalion rested and reorganised.	
	13/10/18		Time devoted to resting, cleaning up and reorganising. Capt L.M.GREENWOOD admitted to hospital.	Effective Strength 15 Off 592 OR. 12 521 OR
	14/10/18		Battalion remained at Premont resting	
	15/10/18		Battalion remained at Premont resting.	
	16/10/18		Lt.Col. P.J. Stone MC joined Battalion and assumed command. Lt W.McBay, Lt J.B.Blythe joined Battalion.	
	17/10/18		Battalion still at Premont. Organised into two companies, 2 "B" team. Draft of 107 ORs arrived	
	18/10/18		Draft of 100 ORs arrived + Lt R.Skelton. Bat'n moved to Maretz and stayed overnight	
	19/10/18		Bat'n moved to HONNECHY. 2Lt H.Leipel, 2Lt Holmes + 2Lt A.M.Mennell joined Battalion.	Effective Strength 29 Off 631 OR
	20/10/18		Battalion in billets at Honnechy. All Lewis Gunners on Range	Ration 17. 606.

Army Form C. 2118.

Page 4 Volume 9
October 1918

WAR DIARY
or
INTELLIGENCE SUMMARY.
(Erase heading not required.)

Place	Date	Hour	Summary of Events and Information	Remarks and references to Appendices
Inchelins	21/10/18		Battn in billets at Honnechy. Training in Open Warfare under Coy arrangements. Relief under on range.	
	22/10/18		Battn in Billets at Honnechy. Draft of 101 ORs arrives. Day spent organising for and attack. Very wet morning. Afternoon spent mostly in Preparation for moving. At Noon heating at 23.30 hrs Battalion marched out of Honnechy towards LE CATEAU and halted one mile N.W. of the town awaiting Zero hour (0170). Tea was served. Battalion shelled and half (?) dig in on road side. B Echelon transport +13 team remained at Honnechy.	
	23/10/18		Battalion moved forward, following up attack by 7th & 73rd Brigades. B Echelon transport +13 team moved from Honnechy to Ponchicourt. Battalion parked through 157 Bde at western edge of Bois L'EVEQUE advanced until they reached road due W of RUE du PONT where they were held up by very heavy machine gun fire and half of same. At 1530 hrs they received orders 9/16 withdraw to the GREENLINE and dig in there for night.	
	24/10/18		The attack was continued, Zero being at 4am the objective being RUE du PONT which was reached by 7.30am. The Battalion Consolidated this position.	

WAR DIARY
or
INTELLIGENCE SUMMARY.

Army Form C. 2118.

Page 5. Volume 9 October 1918

Place	Date	Hour	Summary of Events and Information	Remarks and references to Appendices
In the line	24/10/18		Lt Col. Hone was wounded here. About mid-day orders were received to continue the attack. Zero hour 1400 and objective the high ground E. of LE FAUX. The Battalion consolidated this position by 1730 hrs. Major H.G. Faber took Command of Battalion.	
	25/10/18		Patrols kept in touch with enemy all the day.	
	26/10/18		Situation of Battalion unchanged. Patrol work carried out day and night.	Effective strength – 30 Off. 591 ORs. Platoon strength 16 Off. 445 ORs.
	27/10/18		In the early morning two posts were established in front of our line. One in a house as an O.P. and the other a Lewis Gun Post at junction of tracks. This was done without casualties. Patrol work carried out all day. At night one platoon established itself round the observation post and consolidated there.	
	28/10/18		Orders were received to establish posts on the track running in 9.15.a. Zero was timed for 1700 hr. This track held by enemy, no attack Patrols reported performed until following morning.	Ref. Sheet 57ANW.
	29/10/18		Attack started at 0500 hr by 2 platoons. Platoons on right. They went left flank and 2 fine and rifle fire, the post on left with very heavy machine gun surrounded. They could not advance further, so they withdrew to their original line. Lt WEWALKER was wounded.	

Army Form C. 2118.

Page 6 Volume 9
October 1918.

WAR DIARY
or
INTELLIGENCE SUMMARY.

Place	Date	Hour	Summary of Events and Information	Remarks and references to Appendices
Catillon	29/10/18	(cont)	During the day the Battalion was relieved by 11" Sherwood Foresters and went into support at Rue du Pont. Orders were received that the Brigade would attack following morning but this was cancelled later.	
	30/10/18		Battalion in support at Rue du Pont.	
	31/10/18		Battalion was relieved by 2 Coys of Warwicks at 1400 hours and came back to Camps outside Le Cateau.	

7/11/18

W.W.W. Major
COMDG. 13th (SERV.) Bn. DURHAM L.I. INFTY.

WAR DIARY
or
INTELLIGENCE SUMMARY.

Army Form C. 2118.

13 D 61
Page 1 Volume 11
November 1918

Vol 40

Place	Date	Hour	Summary of Events and Information	Remarks and references to Appendices
In the field	1/11/18		Battn resting near LE CATEAU. Day spent cleaning up - organising into 4 Coys & refitting	
	2/11/18		Morning wet. Boys spent morning arms & Platoon Drill. Afternoon spent Resting. Conference by C.O. at H.Q. in St Benin during afternoon on proposed attack	
			Effective Strength 28 Offrs 656 O.R. Ration " 20 " 587 "	
	3/11/18		Battalion marched to POMMEREUIL where it was billeted for the night. C.O. attended conference at Brigade H.Q.	
	4/11/18	5.45 AM	The battalion moved via the POMMEREUIL - MALGARNI road, and thence by track to road running through G.20.a.9. and G.21.a.7. in support to 74 Bde and consolidated for the night a line E. of the SAMBRE CANAL in G.22.b. Battn HQ established in farm house on Canal at G.22.b.9.6	
	5/11/18		The battalion continued its advance in support to the Bde and crossed the PETITE HELPE RIVER by bridge near MARGOIENNE and took up position for the night in support line E of RUE des JUIFS. During the night battn was relieved and billeted in RUE des JUIFS	

Army Form C. 2118.

Page 2. Volume 11
November 1918

WAR DIARY
or
INTELLIGENCE SUMMARY.
(Erase heading not required.)

Place	Date	Hour	Summary of Events and Information	Remarks and references to Appendices
In the field	5/11/18			
	6/11/18		Drums and transport moved up to LE PRESEAO Advance continued. About mid-day orders were received to advance.	
			The road running through I 13a – C 7d – C 7a – C 8 c+d through TAISNIERES thence by road running S.E. to MARBAIX with the object of capturing this village if not already evacuated. Operation carried out without opposition and MARBAIX entered at 17.00 hours. Heavy shelling met just before entering town and the battalion sustained 10 casualties. Touch obtained with the Yorkshire Regt. and Sherwood Foresters E & S of the town. The battalion was billeted in MARBAIX for the night	
	7/11/18	2-0 PM	The battalion with the rest of the Brigade marched to MARDILLES where it was billeted for the night.	
	8/11/18		Battn marched from MAROILLES to BOUSIES	
	9/11/18		Battalion spent morning in cleaning up + reorganising. Boys and platoon drill	
				Effective strength 28 Officers 854. 6 R's
				Ration strength 21 " " 786 "
	10/11/18		Brigade Church parade in the morning. Afternoon spent in playing off ties of the inter-platoon football competition	

Army Form C. 2118.

Page 3 Volume 11
November 1918

WAR DIARY
or
INTELLIGENCE SUMMARY.
(Erase heading not required.)

Place	Date	Hour	Summary of Events and Information	Remarks and references to Appendices
In the field	11/11/18		Batt'n spent the day in clearing the roads in the area of refuse. Specialists classes for Lewis gunners & signallers were held. Armistice from 11.00 hours was notified.	
	12/11/18		The batt'n was bathed. Training was carried out	
	13/11/18		The batt'n marched to "LE CATEAU". Lt F.H.ALL reported arrival and appointed A/QM	
	14/11/18		CO's inspection and training	
	15/11/18		Kit inspection	
	16/11/18		Training was carried out	Officers strength 28 Officers 9576 R&F Ration strength 20 " 859 "
	17/11/18		Church Parades	
	18/11/18		Battalion Route March. The following Officers reported arrival:- Capt M.J. Morrison M.C., 2/Lt W.T. Donyson, 2/Lt P.T. Lear, 2/Lt J.H. Campbell, 2/Lt A. Argyle, 2/Lt A. Martyr. Capt A.E.B. Howard appointed Bde Transport Officer and struck off the strength of the Battalion	

Army Form C. 2118.

Page 4 Volume 11
November 1918

WAR DIARY
or
INTELLIGENCE SUMMARY.
(Erase heading not required)

Place	Date	Hour	Summary of Events and Information	Remarks and references to Appendices
In the field	19/11/18		Training and Specialist classes. 2/Lt J. Knotts assumed the duties of Transport Officer vice Capt A.E.B. Howard	
	20/11/18		2/Lt R.G. Bear reported arrival. Two boys on Salvage work Two boys training. Lt + 2/Lt Duncan reported arrival. 2/Lt A Martyr admitted to hospital	
	21/11/18		Two boys on Salvage work. Two boys training + Specialist classes	
	22/11/18		Two boys on Salvage work. Two boys training + Specialist classes	
	23/11/18		Two boys on Salvage work. Two boys training + Specialist classes. Effective Strength 34 Officers 959 O.Rs Ration Strength 29 " 845 "	
	24/11/18		Battalion was bathed. Church parades.	
	25/11/18		Two boys on Salvage work. Two boys training + Specialist classes	
	26/11/18		Three boys on Salvage work. One boy training + Specialist classes. 2/Lt R.V. MANNING reported his arrival	

Army Form C. 2118.

WAR DIARY
or
INTELLIGENCE SUMMARY.
(Erase heading not required.)

Page 5 Volume 11
November 1918

Instructions regarding War Diaries and Intelligence Summaries are contained in F. S. Regs., Part II. and the Staff Manual respectively. Title pages will be prepared in manuscript.

Place	Date	Hour	Summary of Events and Information	Remarks and references to Appendices
In the field	27/11/18		All Coys on Salvage work, Specialist classes and lecture on Demobilization	
	28/11/18		All Coys on Salvage work and Specialist classes	
	29/11/18		Battalion marched to ST. HILAIRE	
	30/11/18		General training and Specialist classes. The following Officers reported their arrival:— Capt A.J. Carr-West 2/Lt W.M. Wardle 2/Lt J.L. Wilson 2/Lt J.G. Tarke Effective Strength 40 Officers 966 O.Rs Ration Strength 32 " 827 "	

COMDG: 13th (Serv.) Bn. DURHAM Lt. Infty.
LT. COL.

WAR DIARY
INTELLIGENCE SUMMARY
(Erase heading not required.)

Army Form C. 2118.

Page 1 Volume 12
December 1918

Place	Date	Hour	Summary of Events and Information	Remarks and references to Appendices
In the Field	1/12/18		Church Parade in factory	
	2/12/18		A & B boys on salvage work. C boy firing on range. D boy Route march. PT class under Bde PT instructor	
	3/12/18.		A & B boys on Salvage work. C & D boys Training. All classes as usual.	
	4/12/18.		Morning spent in cleaning up. H.M. The King passed through ST. HILAIRE. Batt paraded @ 13.30 hours to line route.	
	5/12/18.		A + B boys Training C + D. boys Salvage. 125 men attended lecture on Reinstatement problems in morning and on Astronomy.	
	6/12/18		A+B boys Training C+D boys Salvage. Classes. Sigs + Lewis Gun Nos 2	
	7/12/18.		Batt medical inspection A+B boys Training C+D boys Salvage. Presentation of medals by G.O.C. 25 th Div. 1 Platoon under 2/Lt. F.G. Parke attended	Effective Strength 70 offs 772 ORs. Ration " 29 " 873
	8/12/18.		Batt bathed and all blankets disinfected @ Div Baths	

13 D 61
VSR 41

Army Form C. 2118.

Page 2 Volume 12
December 1918

WAR DIARY
or
INTELLIGENCE SUMMARY.
(Erase heading not required.)

Place	Date	Hour	Summary of Events and Information	Remarks and references to Appendices
In the Field	9/12/18		A & B Coys Salvage C & D Coys Route march. Classes:- Buglers + Signallers. Same. Platoon paraded under 2/Lt J.G. Parke for medal presentation by OC 25th Div	
	10/12/18		A & B Coys Salvage C & D Coys COs. inspection 100 Miners interviewed @ Cambrai	
	11/12/18		A & B Coys Salvage C & D Coys Training Signalling + Bugling classes.	
	12/12/18		C & D Coys Salvage A Coy Kit Inspection + Interior Economy. B Coy Route March	
	13/12/18		C & D Coys Route march. b & D Coys Salvage. Specialist Classes commenced. & Education.	
	14/12/18		b & D Coys Salvage A & B Training Specialist Classes.	
			Effective Strength 16 Ofrs 880 ORs.	
			Ration " 17 " 762 "	
	15/12/18		Church Parade in Factory	
	16/12/18		A & B Coys Salvage b & D Coys Inspection + Training. Specialist Classes.	
			2/Lt Jones reported his arrival	
	17/12/18		A & B Coys Salvage. b & D Coys Training + Route march. Specialist classes.	
	18/12/18		A & B Coys Salvage b & D Coys Physical Training + Route march Specialist classes.	
			Capt D.H. Evans RAMC attached to Battalion	
	19/12/18		A C D Coys Salvage. B Coy proceeded to HAUSSY to clean up new billets	
			Specialist + Educational classes.	

Army Form C. 2118.

WAR DIARY
or
INTELLIGENCE SUMMARY.
(Erase heading not required.)

Page 3. Volume 12 December 1918

Place	Date	Hour	Summary of Events and Information	Remarks and references to Appendices
In the Field	20/12/18		3 Coys bathed & moved to HAUSSY.	
	21/12/18		3 Coys Salvage. Coy. Baths.	
			Effective Strength Ofrs. 40. ORs. 795.	
			Ration " 32 " 661	
	22/12/18		Church Parade. Voluntary Divine Service.	
	23/12/18		Salvage. Major A.G. Taber proceeded on leave. Lt./Capt. R.H. Farrier to be A/Capt. whilst commanding a Company.	
	24/12/18		Holiday.	
	25/12/18		Xmas Day. Voluntary Divine Service.	
	26/12/18		Holiday.	
	27/12/18		4 Coys Salvage. Education Class.	
	28/12/18		4 Coys Salvage. Education Class.	
			Effective Strength 38 Ofrs. 596 ORs	
			Ration " 32 " 484 "	
	29/12/18 Sunday		4 Coys Salvage. Day being observed as a workday.	
	30/12/18		Battalion moved to BEAUDIGNIES.	
	31/12/18		Holiday, as Sunday, 29th was observed as a workday.	

W.G. Tabin
Major
13th (SERV.) Bn. DURHAM L.I.

Army Form C. 2118.

WAR DIARY
or
INTELLIGENCE SUMMARY.
(Erase heading not required.)

13th D.L.I. January 1919.

Place	Date	Hour	Summary of Events and Information	Remarks and references to Appendices
O.R.Fields	Jan 1st		Salvage work. Reg't a/c Audited.	
	2nd		Salvage work. Specialist classes.	
	3rd		Salvage work. Battalion bathed.	
	4th		M/c Salvage Work. Training carried out. Kit Inspection. Effective Strength Off 39 O.Rs 589	Ration " 35 " 529
	5th		Sunday. Church Parades. Companies organised into 2 platoons	
	6th		Salvage work. Practice Presentation+trooping of the Colours.	
	7th		Salvage work. Specialist classes. Practice presentation trooping of the colours	
	8th		Capt A.J. Barnley field officer. Salvage work in Phisiques.	
	9th		Salvage work. Practice trooping of the colours 2nd Lt Wellin reported to arrival	
	10th		Salvage work. + Education class.	
	11th		Kit Inspection + practice trooping the colours. Effective Strength 40 Off's 5.96 O.Rs	Ration " 35 " 520
	12th		Church parade.	
	13th		Salvage Work + practice trooping the colours.	
	14th		Salvage Work.	
	15th		Salvage work. Practice trooping the colours.	

COMDG: 13th (SERV.) Bn. DURHAM Lt. INFTY.
LT. COL:

WAR DIARY
or
INTELLIGENCE SUMMARY.

(Erase heading not required.)

Army Form C. 2118.

Summary of Events and Information January 1919

Place	Date	Hour	Summary of Events and Information	Remarks and references to Appendices
N.R. Field Barr.	17th		Salvage work	
	"18th"		Salvage work. O.C. b. inspected the Batts billets. Watched practice trooping the colours	
	19th		by inspected Batts practice trooping colours. Ration effective strength 41 officers 814 o.r's	
	20th		2nd Lt Blake rejoined Battalion. Admitted Hospital same day. Church Parade. Ration " 32 " 5/14	
	21st		Salvage work	
	22nd		6.0. inspection. Practice trooping of the colours 1600. Salvage work	
	23rd		King's Colour Presented to the Battalion by Major Gen. Sir H. Charles. C.B. D.S.O.	
	24th		Salvage work	
	25th		Cairn Baker-Baulds discharged. Court of Enquiry held re-loss of trestles at	
	26th		Salvage work. Lecture given @ Enquiries on Demobilisation & Reconstruction Effective Strength	
				officers 32 536
			Church Parade.	42 492
	27th		Salvage work	
	28th		Salvage work	
	29th		Salvage work. Regt. S/o Audited A Coy non mil Coy. football competition	
	30th		Divine work. C of Enquiry held re accident to C.S.M. T. Robson.	
	31st		Salvage work. Specialist classes 2/Lt T. Hirsch rejoined Battalion. Effective Strength 42 444 O.R.'s 25 393

17 FEB 1919

COMDG: 13th (SERV.) Bn. DURHAM L.I.

Lt. Col.

13 D L J
February 1919
Volume 2. Page 1.
Vol 4.3

WAR DIARY
or
INTELLIGENCE SUMMARY.
(Erase heading not required.)

Army Form C. 2118.

Place	Date	Hour	Summary of Events and Information	Remarks and references to Appendices
Villers-en-Cauchies	1/2/19		Salvage Work. Signalling & Education Classes	
"	2/2/19		Church Parades.	
"	3/2/19		Salvage Work. Lecture for troops at LOUVIGNIES on "South Africa" by Lt Col. O'Blank. 250 mb. returned from hospital.	
"	4/2/19		Salvage Work & Classes as usual.	
"	5/2/19		Salvage Work. Battalion bathed. Lt A Manley returned from hospital	
"	6/2/19		Salvage Work & Specialist Classes.	
"	7/2/19		Salvage Work. Medical Inspection. Battalion formed into 2 Companies	
"	8/2/19		Salvage Work & Specialist Classes. Executive strength 39 off. 3760 Ration — 15 off. 2980	
"	9/2/19		Church Parades.	

Army Form C. 2118.

WAR DIARY
or
INTELLIGENCE SUMMARY.

(Erase heading not required.)

February 1919. Volume 2 Page 2

Place	Date	Hour	Summary of Events and Information	Remarks and references to Appendices
Illiers en Cruchies	10/2/19		Salvage Work.	
"	11/2/19		Salvage Work.	
"	12/2/19		5 Limbers of wood brought from Forêt de Mormal. Graves work continued. 2nd Lieut L.A.B. Allsow returns from leave. 2nd Lieut J.E. Parke takes over Salvage Officer from Lt W.G. Annouman.	
	13/2/19		Graves work. Lt W. Annouman proceeds to England for demobilization. 2nd Lt R.W. Manning rejoins Battalion.	
	14/2/19		2nd Lt J.E. Parke proceeds to England for demobilization. 2nd Lt Manning takes over duties of Salvage Officer. Graves Work continues.	39 O.R. 371 O.R. 19 O.R. 375
	15/2/19		Battalion Bathed. Football match between A&B Coys. Former won 3 goals to 2 goals.	

Army Form C. 2118.

WAR DIARY
or
INTELLIGENCE SUMMARY.

(Erase heading not required.)

February 1919. Page 3
Volume 2.

Place	Date	Hour	Summary of Events and Information	Remarks and references to Appendices
Villers-en-Cauchies	16/2/19		Church parade.	
do	17/2/19		2nd Lieuts Rodgers & Wilson proceeded home for demobilization during demobilization. Horse & Salvage went. H.Q. Coy assembles at Hawvey for trial of H.W. Porter. Major H.Q. Faber proceeds to England to take charge of party for demobilization.	
do	18/2/19		Lower Work cleaning up debris preparatory to move. Capt W. James MC returns from leave.	
do	19/2/19		Battalion moves to Hawvey, arriving at 13.00 hrs.	
do	20/2/19		B attalion moves to Villers-en-Cauchies. Arriving at 12.30 hrs.	
do	21/2/19		Cleaning up & improving of huts.	
do	22/2/19		Cleaning up & improving of huts.	Effective Strength 39 Off. & 381 OR.s. Ration str 31 Off. & 291 OR.s
do	23/2/19		Church parade.	

Army Form C. 2118.

WAR DIARY
or
INTELLIGENCE SUMMARY.
(Erase heading not required.)

February 1919
Volume 2 Page 4.

Place	Date	Hour	Summary of Events and Information	Remarks and references to Appendices
Villers-au-Bouchere	24/2/19		Cleaning up & Improving of billets. Commanding Officer inspected billets.	
do	25/2/19		Salvage Work.	
do	26/2/19		Salvage Work. III Army Inspector of arms visited Battalion inspected Lewis Guns & Rifles. Education Class.	
do	27/2/19		Salvage Work.	
do	28/2/19		Salvage Work. Officers Riding school commenced.	Effective Strength Off 36 OR 324 Ration Strength 19 265

Lt. Col.
COMDG: 13th (SERV.) Bn. DURHAM Lt INFTY.

www.ingramcontent.com/pod-product-compliance
Lightning Source LLC
Chambersburg PA
CBHW081249170426
43191CB00037B/2091